INSPIRE

Courageous People of Our Time

"Courage is rightly esteemed the first of human qualities because it is the quality which guarantees all others."

Sir Winston Churchill

INSPIRE

Courageous People of Our Time

Oliver Chittenden
Foreword by Sir Richard Branson
Portraits by Sam Pelly

in association with The London Speaker Bureau

www.theinspirebook.com
info@theinspirebook.com

First published in 2008
by Oliver Chittenden

Copyright © Oliver Chittenden 2008
Portraits © Sam Pelly and Oliver Chittenden 2008
Text © Oliver Chittenden 2008

The London Speaker Bureau
Elsinore House
77 Fulham Palace Road
London W6 8JA
United Kingdom

Tel: +44 (0)20 8748 9595
E-mail: speakers@londonspeakerbureau.co.uk
www.londonspeakerbureau.co.uk

Sam Pelly Photography
www.sampelly.com

Designed and produced by 8 Books Ltd
www.8books.co.uk

Charities closely associated with each of the people featured in this book have their websites
printed at the end of each essay.

A catalogue record for this book is available from the British Library

ISBN 978 0 9559960 0 9

Printed in Italy on Satimat green (50% recycled) paper by Grafiche Damiani

CONTENTS

We are lucky that our world is full of many incredible people and Oliver's book *Inspire* looks at the lives of some very heroic individuals who all demonstrate a combination of dedication, courage, belief and an acceptance of risk. Throughout my career I have always been inspired by people who show these qualities.

We all have dreams – what the people in *Inspire* have shown is how to follow that dream and turn it into a reality. They are truly inspirational. All of the individuals in this book would describe themselves as "ordinary", but they have an extraordinary gift for achieving and for inspiring others. It is a privilege to read their insights.

Sir Richard Branson

"To think of the immense well of potential hidden deep within our being, to understand that the nature of mind is fundamental purity and kindness, and to meditate on its luminosity, will enable you to develop self-confidence and courage."

The 14th Dalai Lama

Introduction

Throughout my career people have told me that I should keep a diary, detailing some of my experiences as an agent to many of the world's most fascinating individuals.

My work has taken me to many parts of the world in the company of former presidents and prime ministers, business leaders, explorers, sporting heroes, thinkers, authors, and – even better – I get to hear them speak about their views and opinions.

I was always most attracted to those inspirational men and women who really have a story to tell and who have achieved so much, usually against all the odds. Why is it that some people are more successful than others? What is success? What makes a great leader? How does one maintain a level of performance that takes you towards your dream? How do we overcome fear to get to our destination? And how high should we aim?

In this book I have tried to answer these questions by interviewing and spending time with some of the United Kingdom's most inspiring individuals. They all have similar qualities and an unquestionable motivation for life. However one thing I noticed, which is less obvious and that I learnt while writing this book, is that all these people understand what it is like to get to that point of staring fear in the face. Where the majority of us retreat into our comfort zone, these people find a little doorway and move through this fear to attain their goal.

It is that moment, whether deciding to remortgage your house to finance your dream project or business idea, staring down the cliff face of a mountain, or finding that strength from within to fight a battle or win a race, which runs through all these characters. That determination and courage to push through the negative forces and risk so much on a dream is what I admire in them all. It is almost like an adrenaline rush, to reach that point where everything is alive, terrifying, yet knowing that, to get beyond and turn the hard work into reality, you have to step through the doorway and hold your nerve.

Inspire is aimed at motivating readers to live the lives they want, free of fear and restriction. There are valuable lessons and insights that will test your resolve and question your direction but fundamentally the message is a positive one aimed at helping people in a small way to believe a little more in themselves, to go that step further and – most importantly – to smile and enjoy the short journey we take through life.

Oliver Chittenden

"This three-year, 52,000-mile odyssey took intricate planning, 1,900 sponsors, a 52-person team to handle complex communications and iron determination mixed with flexibility. The circumnavigation has never been repeated."

Ranulph Fiennes

Sir Ranulph Fiennes
Global Explorer

Sir Ranulph Fiennes is described as "the world's greatest living explorer" by the *Guinness Book of Records* and his achievements to date show this is no exaggeration.

Following his early military career and his time in the special forces, with both the SAS and the army of the Sultan of Oman, Sir Ranulph has been at the forefront of numerous worldwide expeditions. All of which have been characterised by courage, determination against all the odds and a streak of competitive rebelliousness.

As a young adult, Ran was happier illegally climbing historic buildings than succeeding academically, as well as pursuing his childhood sweetheart and later wife of 36 years, Ginny. This was despite her father's insistence that Fiennes was "Mad, Bad and Dangerous To Know", which he later gave as the title to his best-selling autobiography.

He has travelled to the most dangerous and inaccessible places on earth, almost died, lost nearly half his fingers to frostbite, raised over £12 million for charity and been awarded the Sultan's Bravery medal, a Distinguished Polar Medal and the Order of the British Empire for "human endeavour and charitable services".

He has been an elite soldier, an athlete, a mountaineer, an explorer, a best-selling author and nearly replaced Sean Connery as cinema's James Bond, 007! And despite all this, Fiennes' life shows no sign of slowing down in the 21st century.

Fiennes has led more than 30 expeditions, including, with Charles Burton, the first and only surface polar circumnavigation of the Earth. He was also the first man to reach both poles by surface travel and, with Mike Stroud, the first to cross the Antarctic Continent unsupported.

Above left: Ran on patrol in the Omani southern deserts, 1969.

Above: The longest track – the first unsupported crossing of the Antarctic continent, 1992.

Right: Geoff Newman, Charlie Burton and Ollie Shepard, part of Ran's Transglobe team, on the Arctic Ocean ice in 1977. This was their first experience of travel at minus 50°C.

He also led the team that discovered the lost city of Ubar on the Omani/Yemeni border in 1992, one of his proudest achievements, as well as the first hovercraft expedition up the Nile, the world's longest river, in 1969.

In 2003, only three and a half months after a massive heart attack, a three-day coma and a double bypass, Ranulph Fiennes (along with his explorer friend Mike Stroud) achieved the first 7x7x7 – seven marathons in only seven days on all seven continents – a remarkable feat. At the same time he had to endure the death from cancer of Ginny, his wife, childhood sweetheart, lifelong companion and the support to whom he attributes much of his success. It was indeed their partnership that launched a series of record-breaking expeditions that kept Fiennes ahead of international rivals for three decades. It was Ginny who was often in charge of the support team, risking her own life on several occasions and being awarded the Polar Medal for her bravery and science research work.

In 2004 Fiennes came second in the International North Pole Marathon, and in 2005 he raised £2 million in memory of his wife for the Marie Curie cancer charity through his ascent of Mount Everest. He came within 400 metres of the summit before being forced to abandon his attempt by an attack of angina.

Fiennes' most recent triumph was to climb the North Face of the Eiger, one of the most awesome mountaineering challenges in the world. He has done all this in spite of a lifelong fear of heights, which he resolved to conquer partly to get away and recover from the grief of Ginny's death. He wanted to try and get positive instead of totally negative. If, as Ran says, you do something that grips your attention, which you are very frightened of, it takes your mind off the mental and emotional pain.

Sir Ranulph is undoubtedly one of the most inspirational speakers in the world. By drawing an analogy between nature's most dangerous and difficult challenges and the very real day-to-day business and personal challenges, Sir Ranulph inspires and motivates audiences around the world in a very personal way.

www.mariecurie.org.uk

Above and right: Ran Fiennes climbing the Eiger in 2007.

Q&A

Which of your expeditions are you the most proud of?

It is difficult to single out one particular expedition - they were all pretty different. For staying-power, I searched over a 26-year period, involving 7 major 4-wheel drive desert journeys, for the lost incense city of Ubar, and eventually discovered its location in 1992. The Transglobe Expedition involved both staying-power and determination on behalf of its unpaid 52 team members, who between them raised the necessary £29 million and 1,900 sponsor companies in order to achieve that historic quest. On the other hand, crossing the Antarctic continent with Mike Stroud in 1993 was by far the most physically draining endeavour that I can remember. So in different ways, I can say that I am "most proud of" all these specific expeditions.

Which expedition would you most readily do again?

The hunt for Ubar – mainly because the climate in Arabia is far more pleasant than that in the polar regions.

What has been your strangest experience whilst on expedition?

About 20 years ago I once went with my late wife on a typical rafting expedition down the Grand Canyon. I actually was lying on the side of the big rubber ring at the front of the boat. They turned the engine off, and we were floating. Soon I saw a black duck, which gradually floated toward the front of the boat. There were children on board, so I thought the duck would be a great hit. As it clocked up against the boat, I grabbed at it and found that it was a human head. So I didn't pull in on board – the children wouldn't have liked it. I told the boatman, and he said there's been this guy in the river for five days after a helicopter crash. That sort of excitement never occurs on real expeditions.

What do you say to people who say you are crazy?

I only select individuals for my expeditions who have specific skills and are of a straightforward, non-excitable nature. None of them are crazy in any way, and together we have raised over £12 million for UK charities… not exactly crazy.

How do you cope with failure? Will Mount Everest remain a challenge for you?

Over 42 years of expeditions, some have been huge successes and others dismal failures. I have learnt not to dwell for too long on either, but just to get on attacking the next one.

What cause is closest to your heart? Why?

Having my wife of 36 years, my mother, and two of my three sisters die within two years of each other, I got to know about the Marie Curie Cancer Care charity, and I have been raising funds for them ever since.

How much of what you do is mind over matter?

I sincerely believe in "mind over matter" and practice it when necessary.

Where does your motivation come from?

Like most people, I need to make a living. My chosen path is leading expeditions, so I am motivated to carry on doing just that (until I win the lottery).

What advice do you give to people who are aspiring to live their dreams?

My advice to people wanting to live their dream is encapsulated in a quote from Goethe: "Whatever you can do, or dream you can… begin it".

What does the future look like for you?

I am contemplating an ambitious expedition and I am currently searching for a sponsor for it. When and if I find a sponsor who says yes to supplying the funds I need, then the future will look extremely rosy.

Ran during his attempt to climb Everest in 2008. He got within 400 metres of the summit.

"My admiration for Ranulph Fiennes is unbounded and thank God he exists. The world would be a far duller place without him."

HRH Prince Charles (Patron to many of Sir Ranulph's expeditions)

"Great thinking comes from being liberated from the constraints of curriculum."

Tim Smit

Tim Smit
Environmentalist

Whilst at Durham University in pursuit of a "Sherlock Holmes" career, studying
Anthropology and Archaeology, Tim Smit formed a rock band. Full of confidence
after a series of successful student concerts, he moved to London just as the punk rock
scene was exploding. With the competition to get a record deal as ruthless as the
industry itself, he soon found himself as an out-of-work musician on the dole, playing
football on Clapham Common.

Typically, Tim Smit found a way around the conventional routes to getting a deal
and was soon writing and producing songs for some of the biggest names in the rock
world, such as Barry Manilow and the Nolan Sisters, and – uniquely at the time –
doing deals direct with recording studios.

Having begun life as a disenchanted archaeology student, Smit spent the next 10
years as a hugely successful composer and producer in the music industry before, as he
says, deciding to "do a Captain Oates and leave" which, he reflects, was his greatest
contribution to music.

Tim originally moved to Cornwall to set up a recording studio away from the greed
and dishonesty of the London music industry. Soon after he arrived there, he made a
decision to lead his life purely on instinct and not to fall victim to the evils of
negativity, no matter how foolish his plans or dreams seemed. He soon developed a
passion for rearing rare pigs which led him to ask a local landowner if he had any land
to rent. They became friends and this led to an invitation from the landowner to visit a
nearby estate he had just inherited which had been neglected for many years and

Above: Tim at the open quarry
before work began on the Eden
Project.

Right: Panoramic aerial view of
the entire Eden Project.

"The closer you get to the obstacle blocking your dream, the longer you hold your nerve, the sooner you will find an opening that makes your dream a reality."

Tim Smit

"Incredible… I am instantly transported back to the rain forest and your mind goes into jungle mode."

Ray Mears

needed a huge amount of money for restoration.

Armed with machetes, together they uncovered on the estate the remains of sumptuous gardens dating back to the 12th century. Tim instantly fell in love with them, despite knowing little about plants, and the idea for The Lost Gardens of Heligan was born. Tim knew that if he could inject his passion, belief and entrepreneurial spirit into this discovery then he could create a fairytale place for the public to enjoy. After two years' restoration, his creation became the subject of a television documentary and, with 350,000 visitors a year, one of the country's top tourist attractions.

At the heart of the fabulous walled gardens are historic glasshouses rescued from overgrowth and total dereliction and now restored to full functionality. In tribute to the generation of staff lost in the Great War, the gardens continue to be worked by hand, utilising the best of past practices.

Tim embraces risk and has an incurable optimism which is very infectious to those around him, making him the ideal team leader. He believes he has a gift for giving others faith in themselves and he takes great pleasure in seeing people whose confidence has been shattered rebuild their excitement in life and rediscover their talents.

There is no doubt that, as well as being a life-changing event, The Lost Gardens of Heligan paved the way for Tim's next undertaking, the Eden Project, which really was his masterpiece in terms of scale and vision.

Only Tim Smit could recognise the potential in a disused, sterile clay pit that was perceived locally as rather ugly and depressed. He saw it as a prime development area and understood the regenerative potential of his scheme. While Tim knew that his plan would benefit the whole area, he also realised that he would require iron will and huge motivation to win over the local people who would be needed to help turn his dream of Eden into a reality.

Tim then tried to persuade the government, which was at the time investing heavily in garden developments around the country, to back a garden festival that he was organising in the clay pits of Cornwall. The politicians were pessimistic, having had too many recent projects that built up the aspirations of the local community only to end in disappointment around a year later.

Despite this, Tim pursued his vision of building the eighth Wonder of the World in this clay pit in Cornwall and, despite being told numerous times that his ambition was far too big for the West Country, he continued winning people over until he got his lucky break, when the best-known British transparent dome designer agreed to take on his project. This gave Tim and his small fighting team a lot of confidence and soon the government reversed its initial decision and decided to give £40 million of National Lottery money to the Eden Project.

Tim is emphatic that his success in getting the Eden Project off the ground was attributable to his ability to talk to civil servants and private investors in a direct and passionate way – to sell the story of the future and make them realise that to not be part of this historic event would be a major lost opportunity.

Tim's humble mission is to tell the world the story of plants that changed history, and with this message he has succeeded in spearheading a campaign which turned a pit into a paradise.

The Eden Project boasts a collection of hexagonal eco-bubbles, massive greenhouses encapsulating Mediterranean landscapes, tropical rainforests and what Smit calls "a living theatre of plants" – at the last count, 250,000 of them. The scale and beauty of his vision cannot fail to impress.

Left: Visitors enjoying the Outdoor biome with external view of the Tropical biome in the background.

Above: Bee and bulbs at the
Eden Project, Cornwall.

Above: WEEE (Waste from Electrical and Electronic Equipment) Man by Paul Bonomini, representing the amount of electrical waste from one human in a lifetime.

Eden began as a dream in 1995 and opened its doors to the public in 2000, since when more than six million people have come to see what was once a sterile pit turned into a cradle of life containing world-class horticulture and startling architecture symbolic of human endeavour. Eden is proud of its success in changing people's perception of the potential and application of science by communicating and interpreting concepts through the use of art, drama and storytelling as well as in taking a pivotal role in local regeneration. The Eden Project demonstrates once and for all that sustainability is not about sandals and nut cutlets, it is about good business practice and the citizenship values of the future.

With children spending less and less time outdoors, Smit understands that in order to protect our planet we have to educate future generations about its needs. Not only are children missing out on fun but there are serious effects including obesity and other health problems as well as negative consequences for the environment and society. At Eden, Smit has developed a charity programme to combat the alienation of children from the environment called "Mud Between Your Toes" which has seen fantastic results.

Eden has provided challenges for even the scarily undaunted Smit. Complex finances and pioneering drainage systems are just two aspects of turning 900,000 tonnes of clay into fertile earth. He has also faced a royalty lawsuit from his original collaborator, but his chin remains high. He says: "If you are already perceived as a maverick, which I am, stuff like this doesn't damage you".

Such stuff, then, is small, probably organic, potatoes for a man whose mission is a major ecological statement – to change the world into one where

"plants provide a canvas on which we can paint an optimistic future".

The first reaction Smit wants from visitors to Eden is "a big wow"; he then aims to educate and fascinate in equal measure. It seems that, for this dynamic botanical guru, not all his entertainment instincts have been left in the recording studio.

On the environmental issues of today, Smit remains optimistic and believes that, if we humans are as wise a race as we think, then we will reverse the problems we have caused. If we do not, then we will become just a footnote in history. It is a challenge that he relishes and one that ultimately comes down to each and every one of us: we must take responsibility and elect the right political and corporate leaders who are courageous enough to take the decisions on the environment that are required. Tim highlights food security as an even greater challenge, with capacity on the shelves of British supermarkets sufficient to feed the population for only two and a half days – we must do more to grow and source food and energy supplies at home rather than become reliant on overseas suppliers. Genuine courage in politicians is very rare. Were Smit to be prime minister, he would make Britain self-sufficient in energy within three years through massive public expenditure – if that came to pass, he would certainly relish the inevitable recognition as a political saviour!

www.edenproject.com

"Aim high even if you hit a cabbage."

Tanni Grey-Thompson

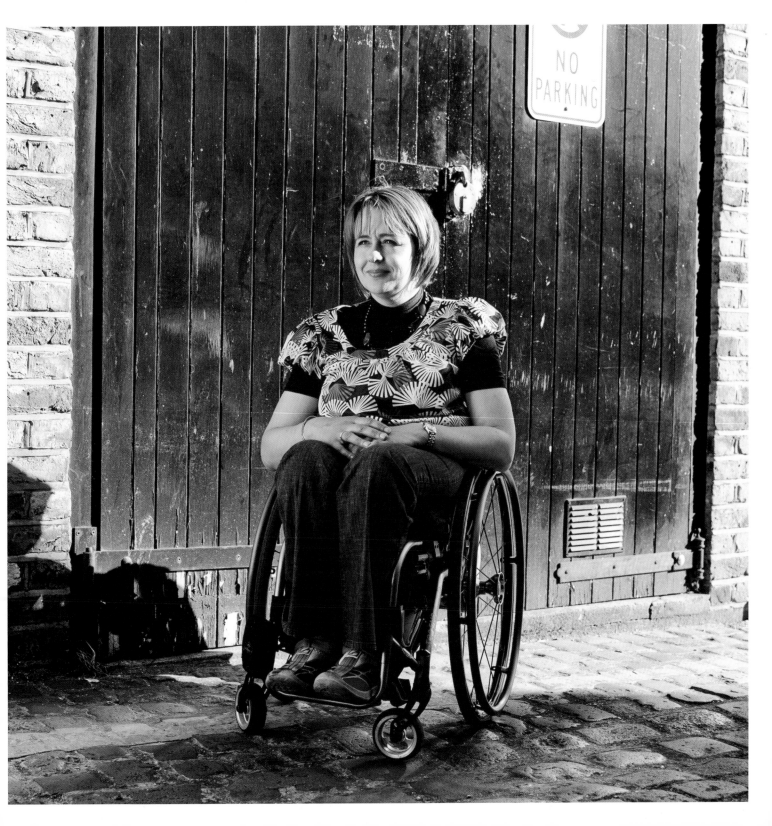

Tanni Grey-Thompson

Paralympian

Tanni Grey-Thompson was born with spina bifida and does not remember the day she got her first wheelchair because it was not important. For Tanni, having a chair simply meant she had better mobility. Her attitude has always been not to look at her limits but instead to try and figure out how to do things to the best of her ability. There is very little that she is unable to do, thanks to her strong will and determination to lead a normal life, free of self-pity.

Tanni Grey-Thompson is Britain's most successful Paralympian and she has forged a remarkable career in athletics from unpromising beginnings. She has also helped to bring disabled sport back into the mainstream, raising the profile of disabled athletes around the world. The incident she most enjoys talking about was when the BBC failed to provide a ramp at the Sports Personality of the Year Awards, where Tanni was due to collect a trophy. This oversight by the BBC propelled disability sport into the headlines and ended up raising awareness in a way that any number of gold medals could never have done. Tanni was neither angry nor bitter that her big night was marred; instead she was delighted to see disability thrust into the spotlight and found it all very amusing.

That the Paralympic profile at the Beijing Olympics will be unrecognisable from that in Seoul in 1988 is partly down to a woman who, against her wishes, has often been used as a media spokeswoman on disability issues. It is why she gave 22 interviews in one day when Glenn Hoddle made his infamous remarks about disabled people paying for sins committed in previous lives, which resulted in him losing his job as England Football Manager.

Tanni first tried wheelchair racing at St Cyres Comprehensive School, in her native Cardiff, aged 13. At 15, she shocked everyone by winning the 100 metres at the Junior National Wheelchair Games. At 18, Tanni joined the Bridgend Athletics Club and was selected by the British Wheelchair Racing Squad for her first World Wheelchair Games.

A year later, in 1988 at Seoul, Tanni represented Britain and won her first Paralympic medal, the 400-metre bronze. Soon after this Tanni was forced away from the track for a year due to spinal surgery but incredibly, at the 1992 Barcelona Paralympics, she stormed to victory taking four gold medals in the 100, 200, 400 and 800 metres. In the same year, she also won her first of six London Wheelchair Marathons.

Despite some hard soul-searching in the weeks after she returned from Atlanta, Tanni realised that she was not ready to retire and instead became determined to prove people wrong. She threw herself into training and returned at the Sydney Paralympics with a vengeance, striking gold four times. Again at Athens in 2004, aged 35, she took gold in the 100 and 400 metres, bringing her Paralympic medal tally to an astonishing 11 gold medals.

Tanni's family have always been incredibly supportive, encouraging her from a young age to try different sports. Where they met obstacles they would fight as a unit to make things possible, as for example when they kept Tanni in mainstream education despite accessibility problems for her wheelchair. Tanni was extremely fortunate to find an outstanding coach at an early stage of her career. She trained with Roy Anthony at Bridgend, and has fond memories of racing down the local multistorey car park in winter when the track was frozen.

Above left: Tanni with one of her Paralympic gold medals from Athens in 2004.

Above right: Tanni, on the left, racing through the Tyne Tunnel.

"I always enjoyed training. I just thought training was part of my life and I knew that if I trained hard then I could race well. My training consisted of two sessions, for six days a week, 50 weeks of the year, including Christmas and my wedding day! I have been lucky throughout my career that I never had any real injuries or illnesses. My lowest time in sport came after the Atlanta Paralympics. I had won one gold and three silver medals but a lot of people, including some of the team and staff, concluded that I was finished and I should retire."

Tanni Grey-Thompson

Right: In the build up to the Paralympics Tanni would train on her local roads. She is seen here on the Jedburgh Road in Northumberland.

Q&A

What motivated you towards athletics and marathons?

I remember watching the disabled athlete Chris Hallam, a Welshman, win the London Marathon in 1984. He had flowing blonde hair and raced in a leopard-print suit – I thought he looked really cool, he was quite outspoken but very inspiring.

How important was winning gold medals to you?

Medals are important to me of course, but more important is the way I raced. Even if I had won a gold medal I would analyse the race afterwards to see if there was any way I could improve my performance for the next race.

How did you prepare for a big race?

I am a perfectionist, so I would always arrive early for a race and get into my racing chair really early. I never spoke to anyone else in a call room before a race, and before every race I was always sick, lots of times.

Would you like to have been competing at the Beijing Paralympics?

I think that my body told me two years ago that it was time to stop – my shoulders are damaged from years of racing, and on a very cold winter's day in the northeast I realised that I didn't really want to carry on. I think it will be a great Paralympics in Beijing, the UK has some fine athletes, and it will be interesting to see how many athletes have come through from the home nation.

Staying at the top in sport takes major commitment. What attributes are required in your experience?

I think I have always been very competitive, which helps. I am also meticulous about planning, so my training was always planned well in advance. Being an international athlete is quite a lonely life, so if you like your own company it is a bonus as there are some long days cooped up in hotel rooms.

What have you been up to since your last Paralympics in Athens?

I retired in 2007, and since then I have become a non-executive director of UK Athletics. I still do motivational speaking and I am involved in a clothing firm called Rackety's who produce adaptive clothing for wheelchair users. I am pretty busy!

Who is your biggest inspiration?

My late mother was always an inspiration to me. I find myself now saying things to my daughter Carys that my mother used to say to me.

What are you most afraid of?

Articulated lorries driving too close when I am on my handbike.

What quality do you admire most in people?

Honesty. Over the years I have relied on my close circle of friends and family to be as honest as possible. They have been my hardest critics but also my staunchest supporters and people I can rely on totally.

What is your next big challenge?

I have just completed my first triathlon, and I really enjoyed it, so I am going to train a bit more to try and complete another next year. I wasn't last, but would like to improve my position next year.

"There is this perception that walking is good and not walking is bad. For me that is not true because being in a wheelchair has given me more mobility, not less. It's different for the guy who falls off a ladder and breaks his back. He's been able to walk and, all of a sudden, he can't. He has had something taken away. That was not the case for me and it has never stopped me doing anything I wanted to do."

Tanni Grey-Thompson

Tanni's husband, Ian, has been a huge support, looking after their daughter Carys and spending a good deal of time helping Tanni with the technical aspect of her training, as well as remembering to keep his distance from Tanni and her pre-race nerves – Tanni is well known for episodes of being sick on the track prior to big races!

Ian was a cyclist until he had a horrible accident involving a lorry which left him in a wheelchair with a broken back. He and Tanni share the same attitude: "Why worry about something you cannot change?"

It has been a long road for Tanni, who as a child was once taunted with the nickname "Limpy Legs". Tanni does not see herself as courageous or as someone who has overcome adversity against the odds. In Sydney, the Paralympics was marketed as a sporting event, pure and simple. Nobody was asking what you had overcome in your disability, instead the Australians had the more refreshing approach of asking what you had to overcome as an athlete. Disability is treated and recognised differently by different cultures around the world and there remains much work to be done on raising awareness in this area, something to which Tanni now devotes much of her time.

As she embarks on life outside athletics with her daughter and husband, this all-time great British woman and purveyor of minor miracles just wants to be remembered as a good athlete and a nice person.

www.zoes-place.org.uk

"Perhaps the point of living is not to be placid and happy and untouched by the world, but to be deeply, painfully sensitive to it, to see its cruelty and savagery for what they are, and accept all this as readily as we accept its beauty. To be touched by it, moved by it, hurt by it even, but not be indifferent to it."

John Simpson

John Simpson
Foreign Correspondent

From an early age, John Simpson was fascinated by adventure, writing and travelling. Looking back, if someone had actually told him that he should be a foreign correspondent it would have made perfect sense but he actually fell into journalism completely by chance.

John started at the very bottom of the BBC chain and gradually made his way up through the ranks to become a reporter and eventually a foreign correspondent. A job that he feels particularly privileged to have, with foreign correspondents slowly becoming a threatened sub-species in today's world, as newspapers and TV channels reduce their overheads. Despite this, journalists in the BBC and elsewhere have come to accept that, where a big story is breaking, John Simpson will probably be there first – his remarkable gut instincts and natural talent for being in the right place at the right time have drawn him into the thick of the action over and over again.

For John, curiosity and a certain determination are the essential elements in becoming a successful reporter. Doors are very rarely opened and no one really wants to invite you in, so dealing with disappointment is an everyday requirement. Curiosity, as well as a desire to tell other people what is going on, are the fundamental drivers to successful reporting.

John Simpson knows his own mind and through his experience has his own independent views on what is going on in the world. He does not need to read newspapers or listen to politicians, he has been able to form his own opinions through his extensive travel and first-hand knowledge of what is happening on the front line of

Above left: John Simpson reporting from Afghanistan. He was one of the first reporters to enter Kabul in 2001 after the US-led invasion of the country.

Above right: John in Northern Iraq during the Second Gulf War in 2003. He was injured in a so-called friendly fire incident when a US plane bombed the convoy he was in, leaving him deaf in one ear.

"This is just a scene from hell here. All the vehicles are on fire. There are bodies burning around me, there are bodies lying around, there are bits of bodies on the ground. This is a really bad own goal by the Americans."

John Simpson

any big story or country. This confidence breeds good reporting as it enables John to be better equipped than most in interviewing people who may try to disguise the truth. He is able to disagree or question information that is passed to him from the highest sources which makes his reporting style unique, challenging, unbiased and above all honest in its determination to convey to the public the truth of what is actually going on. With so many lies and exaggerations being spun around the media, it makes John Simpson's open, honest and old-fashioned style of reporting even more important in communicating the truth to the public.

Throughout John's career he has been concerned about human rights and it is amongst his priorities to contribute to the absolute right of people to have access to free and honest information. Bringing to light evidence of human rights' abuses around the world has been fundamental to John's motivation in reporting and hence allowing people to be freer in what they say, do and think.

In the past, great states such as the former Soviet Union, China and many African countries prevented people from saying what they believed to be true. The world has changed since then and there are fewer dictators around the world. As John points out, the threat now comes more from within our own society where people are not sufficiently aware of the need to be interested in what is going on in the world. This ignorance is as much a form of censorship as silencing people with the butt of a rifle if they speak out of turn.

The defining moment of John Simpson's career was witnessing the collapse of the Soviet Empire. He was reporting from Czechoslovakia, where crowds of people were pouring onto the streets, growing in numbers day by day as their confidence grew, to demonstrate against a vicious, brutal and corrupt government. It was this sheer moral

Above left: John Simpson and fellow BBC journalist Fergal Keane.

"In my dream I lay in a gutter, sheltering from the bombs. The only time I have taken shelter in a gutter was in June 1989, during the massacre of Tiananemen Square. I threw myself down that night; and, I promise you, a kerbstone gives remarkably little cover from bullets. Perhaps that, rather than the bombing, was what disturbed my sleep."

Extract from John Simpson's book *Not Quite World's End*

force of a people and an irresistible demand for freedom and openness that resulted in the overthrow of a government and an Empire. What made this even more historic was that it was achieved not through shooting people, burning and looting, suicide bombs and explosives, but through the peaceful voice of the people.

Five years later, whilst reporting on the election that Nelson Mandela won in South Africa, John Simpson witnessed again the sight of people taking their freedom peacefully through pure moral force after what was a brutal Apartheid system of pain, violence and destruction. John recognises that these things do not necessarily last, as with Russia's resurgence, with the old Soviet Empire looking rather tired and sick today. And South Africa is not what we all hoped it would be back in 1994. But these key moments for democracy will and should never be forgotten. That you do not need to kill other people to change things, but can do this through the simple, courageous exercise of your own right to speak out and think for yourself, is possibly the most valuable lesson to be learned from these defining moments in history.

John Simpson's opposition to the aggression, violence and destruction that he has witnessed regularly in Iraq and Afghanistan or indeed on the streets of London has shaped his view of the world. Whether it comes in the form of a suicide bomber or an American fighter jet, this disregard for human life is something that upsets him deeply.

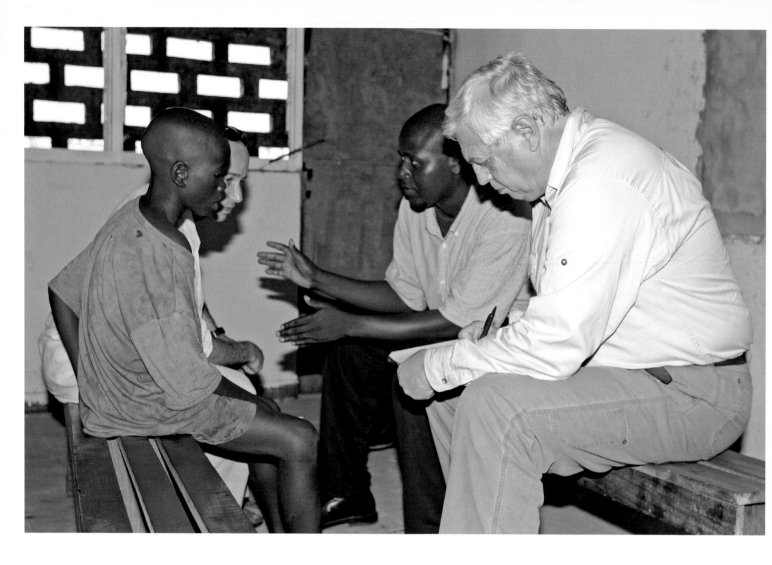

Above: John Simpson interviewing child "wizards" in the Democratic Republic of Congo in 2006.

> "This is not an easy job, you have to find a foot in the door. It is much like being a Jehovah's Witness or an encyclopedia salesman, nobody really wants you around or actively invites you in."

John Simpson

Becoming a father again at the age of 62 has sensitised John even more to the importance of human life. His young son often stands at the doorway of his house with his hands held up trying to block his father's departure on yet another trip to report from the front line. Although very upsetting, John believes it is important for his boy to see his parents being active and he remains adamant that it is perfectly possible to be over 60 with white hair and a lived-in face, and still be immensely active.

In a career which makes visiting trouble spots a way of life, John says he rarely fears for his safety, despite having been subjected to a mock execution in Lebanon and, more recently, to a "friendly fire" incident in Iraq, when an anti-tank bomb was dropped and detonated a few yards from him, killing his translator and showering John with shrapnel.

Other close shaves include being shelled in Afghanistan, attacked with poisonous gas in the Gulf and dodging bullets in Tiananmen Square. John also had the honour as a young reporter of being punched by Harold Wilson for asking whether he was about to call an election.

There is no question that, in a BBC career spanning 40 years, John has earned a reputation as one of the world's most experienced and authoritative journalists.

www.amnesty.org

"Live boldly, follow your dreams, take risks, look after your friends and smile when the mountain is steepest…"

Bear Grylls

Bear Grylls

Professional Adventurer

A great deal of Bear's inspiration in life comes from his late father, who taught him to climb at a very young age and also instilled in him the courage to live out his dreams, no matter how mad they may be.

For Bear, climbing began as a way of bonding with his father; as he became more confident, it became an end in itself. It was not long before Bear was climbing church spires at school, feeling more challenged by this type of activity than by achieving academically. Bear's childhood ambition to climb Mount Everest became his ultimate goal, and was totally in tune with his father's message of "Live your dreams".

Two years before his ascent of Everest, Bear suffered a near-fatal parachuting accident. Whilst serving with the SAS in Africa, he broke his back in three places and narrowly escaped being paralysed. Following months of rehabilitation in an army hospital, Bear slowly built up his strength, motivated even more by this accident to achieve his dream of scaling the world's highest mountain. With typical determination and charm, Bear fought hard to regain full mobility and, together with a team of friends, planned his expedition and raised the necessary sponsorship to face this daunting challenge.

Every year, Everest claims new victims: one in every ten mountaineers who try to climb it dies in the attempt. On 26 May 1998, at the age of only 23, Bear Grylls became the youngest Briton to scale the peak. During the 90-day climb, he endured extreme weather conditions and sleep deprivation and ran out of oxygen deep inside the "death zone" (above 26,000 feet). On the way down from his first reconnaissance

Above: Bear during his ascent of Everest in 1998.

Right: In 2003 Bear successfully completed the groundbreaking expedition of leading a team across the North Atlantic Ocean in an inflatable open boat.

"Mick was literally washed off his seat, and the force of the water threw him on top of me. We both clutched at anything solid around us. In the dark, and in blind panic, I grabbed hold of the wheel again and frantically tried to guess where the next freak wave was coming from. We were like blind men in a boxing ring. Alone and afraid."

Bear Grylls, *Facing the Frozen Ocean*

climb, Bear cheated death while negotiating the perilous Khumbu Icefall: the ice cracked and he fell into a 1,000 feet crevasse; he was knocked unconscious and had it not been for the tenacity of his team mates he would not be alive today.

Bear attributes much of his strength to his Christian faith. That, together with his family, provides him with the anchor for the courage to continue living his dreams, taking risks and going on expeditions. For Bear, it is in those life-and-death situations that he feels most alive; existence then becomes much more raw and focused. Bear understands what is important and does not get carried away by the fluff of city-dwelling and commercial gains. He is adamant that the way we act now is how we define ourselves in difficult times. Whilst recognising that life is full of challenges and troubles, no matter what we are doing, we must be bold and think big. As Bear says, he is not a particularly talented climber or athlete, but by taking risks and committing himself, where others have fear, he has grown, whilst remaining humble enough to recognise that there are many more heroic people out there on the front line working these same physical skills to save lives everyday. This way of thinking may not encourage an easy road but it will make life exciting and fulfilling. At a time when we are under so much pressure to be money-driven, status-driven and commercially minded, Bear believes the magic exists not on the well-trodden paths but "off piste" and he encourages his audiences and people in general to search out these experiences and not to be slaves to the shallow master of commercialism.

Commitment to an expedition is key to its success. It is being tentative and holding back that makes things go wrong, as with a rugby tackle – if you hesitate you are much more likely to get injured. Bear continues to be goal-driven and lives off these life-defining moments and dreams. When he commits to something, that is when things fall into place. He may win or lose but he understands this track and, with his family and faith behind him, the sky really is the limit to his dreams.

Right: Bear's television survival programmes, including *Man vs Nature* and *Born Survivor*, have become hugely popular.

Left: Bear in typically adventurous form. He has stated that it is in life-and-death situations that he really feels most alive.

At the end of your life, what do you want to leave behind you as a legacy?
To have touched people's lives and to have encouraged many to not be scared to follow their dreams.

How do you overcome your fear of heights?
I take my time, check my safety and remind myself that most fears are irrational and then I just get on with it!

What is the best survival tool to carry with you besides a knife, flint and canteen?
Our brain is our greatest survival tool – survival is all about ingenuity: thinking your way around a challenge, calmly, in the heat of the moment. And a big heart is then needed to keep going and to never give up.

Where are you happiest?
Lying in the long grass, in the sun, on our Welsh hideaway with my family. No phones, no nothing but family cosiness.

What is going through your head when you are paragliding over Everest or facing imminent danger in the wild?
You are in the moment – that is the magic. Nothing clouds you – life is reduced to just life – no fluff. It is summed up by the phrase "Everest… by God's grace".

What did your time with the Special Forces teach you?
To be able to look after myself and those around me when the chips are down and it is all turning nasty. It gave me confidence in my own ability that I did not always have growing up.

Which adventurer do you admire most and why?
Ran Fiennes. He has helped and encouraged me so much. Quite a father figure to me, I feel very small when I compare myself to this true champion of exploration. Ran has always used his expeditions to raise funds and awareness for charities and we both know we have a great opportunity to make a difference to people's lives – that is in itself a privilege.

"If I go up to the heavens, you are there;
if I make my bed in the depths, you are there.

If I rise on the wings of the dawn,
if I settle on the far side of the sea,

even there your hand will guide me,
your right hand will hold me fast."

Psalm 139: 8–10

In 2003 Bear successfully completed another groundbreaking expedition, leading a team across the North Atlantic Ocean in a small rigid inflatable open boat. Powered by a revolutionary fuel made from waste materials, the boat and crew took a battering from frozen spray and icebergs. The journey was often even more life-threatening than his experiences on the face of Everest. The expedition was filmed for a documentary and raised substantial funds for the Prince's Trust charity. Bear's account of the expedition, *Facing the Frozen Ocean*, followed his first book, *Facing Up*, about his ascent of Mount Everest. In both works, the writing touched people through its enduring honesty, courage and humility.

In 2007, Bear became the first man to fly a powered paraglider above Mount Everest raising over $2.5 million for children's charities worldwide and this, combined with his other achievements, led him to become a popular TV adventure presenter. He is currently filming the hugely popular documentary *Man vs Wild / Born Survivor: Bear Grylls*, which sees him being parachuted into some of the most inhospitable deserts, jungles and mountains on earth while displaying the skills required to survive. This reaches a global audience of over 1 billion viewers.

www.globalangels.org

"There is too much hatred in this world and children are the innocent victims. Having witnessed its destructive consequences on humanity I am convinced that love is the only power that can defeat it."

Mark Cook

Colonel Mark Cook

Humanitarian

Colonel Mark Cook, a soldier with the Gurkhas for over 30 years, was on a tour of duty as commander of the British United Nations Contingent in the former Yugoslavia when he came across a shattered Croatian orphanage. The sight of 60 orphaned children, victims of the Balkan War, touched him so deeply that he promised the children he would rebuild it.

The plight of these children and the destruction he witnessed were to change the course of his life. With little idea of how to go about raising the necessary funds and having been advised that the orphanage would cost nearly £1 million to rebuild, he flew down to Sarajevo to discuss the matter with Martin Bell, an old school friend who was then the BBC correspondent in the region.

In what was to become typical of his courage and determination to help orphans affected by war around the world, Mark met Martin Bell in the heart of the front line. Whilst there, a gun battle broke out in downtown Sarajevo and Martin told everyone to jump into his armour-plated Land Rover, which he had fondly named "Miss Piggy". Before Mark knew what was happening they found themselves in the middle of a fierce exchange of fire between Serbs and Muslims. It soon became apparent that they had become the targets and, as Martin was reaching for body armour to put on over his trademark white suit, a mortar bomb struck. Martin took multiple shrapnel wounds to the stomach. Mark recalls how impressed he was with the BBC warfare training, as, with the cameras still rolling, Martin reported: "I've been hit, I am alive, I will survive".

"Mark's speciality is hopeless causes and impossible missions. It is a striking exhibition, amid the chaos and anarchy of the new world order, of the difference one man can make. Mark Cook is such a man."

Martin Bell, BBC War Correspondent

One hour later, as Martin was being operated on in the military hospital, Mark was asked by the BBC to fill his slot on the One O'Clock News. With Big Ben sounding in his ear and a gun battle going on in the background, Mark seized the opportunity of being live on TV to explain what he was doing in Sarajevo and his plea to raise £1 million for the orphanage reached a global audience. Mark soon realised that he could not keep his promise to the children whilst he was in the Army. So, he resigned his commission and 18 months later the building was complete and the children returned to their new home.

Soon afterwards Mark, together with his wife, Caroline, revisited Sarajevo to investigate the terrible conditions orphans were being subjected to in this besieged city. To get back to the front line they managed to obtain media passes that enabled them both to reach the heart of Sarajevo. Awaiting them there were the most terrible, disgusting conditions imaginable.

This is when Mark and Caroline decided that something had to be done about these desperate children. Again Mark gathered all the children and, using his interpreter, told them that they would rebuild their orphanage. It took many trips to convince these battle-hardened children and the staff that he meant it and most importantly to gain their trust.

So at the age of 50, having been a part of one loving family while growing up and then of another with his army regiment, instead of retiring to the golf course, Mark

Above left: Caroline and Mark Cook in Sudan.

> # "The greatest poverty on this earth is not the lack of food but the lack of love."
>
> **Mother Teresa**

and his devoted wife Caroline set up the charity Hopes and Homes for Children.

Now in its 15th year, this inspirational charity has helped children in 15 of the poorest countries in the world, including Rwanda, Sierra Leone, Sudan, Bosnia and Romania .Together, this courageous couple have given everything to achieve their mission of bringing hope to the poorest children in the world – those who are orphaned, abandoned or vulnerable – by enabling them to grow up within the love of a family and the security of a home, so that they can fulfil their potential.

Sierra Leone was the first African country they started working in, having been drawn there by chance when Caroline accepted a reverse charge telephone call from a teacher there making a plea for help. Three weeks later they flew out and found themselves in the middle of another war where the children were being abused in terrible ways; many small children had their limbs amputated by the rebels as a method of striking fear in the local people, young boys were forced to kill and girls used as sex slaves. Initially they rented a big house from a Paramount Chief to shelter 35 orphaned children and by the end of the war, five years later, they found themselves helping over 600 children who had lost their homes and families.

What Mark and Caroline quickly realised is that there are millions of children in this world whose lives are on a knife-edge and the odds are stacked against them, with many having to resort to begging, crime and prostitution just to survive. However, with a little bit of help these children's lives can be changed from potentially negative forces in society to positive ones. They went out and asked many children in various countries what they really wanted more than anything else. The answer was always the same, regardless of race, colour or creed: "Please give me a family. I want a home." When they asked one little boy in Sudan what he thought a home was, he responded immediately "a home is love."

As Mark Cook says, there are more orphans in the world now than ever before in history. In modern wars, 85% of casualties are civilians so there are many more children with no one to look after them and they become totally vulnerable. With the ever increasing problems of AIDS and conflict in Africa, UNICEF estimates that by 2010 there will be 25 million orphans in sub-Saharan Africa alone, most of whom will not stand a chance and will grow up falling into an abyss of despair.

The Cooks of this world do not think grandly, as political leaders, of Africa as a challenge that can only be resolved given the will and enough money by the West. They see it differently, having been given their purpose by that simple message from the

> "The candle Mark and Caroline have lit seems to offer a precious little light in the darkness that threatens to envelop many of the world's children. But if others light similar candles, it will grow less dark. There is no knowing what the love Hope and Homes for Children seeks to arouse in the human heart might achieve in a hard world."

Lord Deedes

children themselves that they want the love and security of a family in their own home. They believe that the world must realise that this is a crisis on an unprecedented scale as these children will grown up to be disenfranchised, angry adults.

Hope and Homes for Children, the charity that Mark and Caroline started 15 years ago, has already touched the lives, either directly or indirectly, of countless thousands of children. Specialised skills that they have learnt are now recognised by many governments and such organisations as UNICEF and the WHO, and they are being asked to help transform outdated, institutionalised childcare systems to ones based on family care. So, they no longer build orphanages, but are helping to close them down and reintegrate children, wherever possible, with their own families or foster families within their own countries. As Mark says,

"understanding where we come from is a core part of what makes us who we are, and families are at the heart of this providing children with a sense of belonging, a unique identity and an anchor in life."

As long as Mark and Caroline are fit and healthy, their mission to help where they can will continue; Mark regards himself as an ambassador for these children and believes he can make a difference by giving them a voice and by encouraging compassion from privileged people and world leaders. They now know that they can touch the lives of millions of children in the future by working together with governments and other agencies

www.hopeandhomes.org

Above: A Romanian child.

"One of my favourite questions I ask of people is 'How do you want to be remembered?' I am not only referring to whether they want to be winners or not but I ask them to think about the overall contribution that they may make to the success of the team."

Sir Clive Woodward

Sir Clive Woodward

Coach

After graduating from Loughborough University with a sports science degree, Clive then spent a year qualifying as a teacher. It was these teaching skills, alongside his degree and business experience with Xerox, that were to prove pivotal in his ability to communicate effectively; communication being a quality to which Clive attributes much of his success as a coach.

The game of rugby had not turned professional when Clive was playing for both England and the British Lions. Most people involved at the highest level had to juggle their professional lives alongside the amateur game. It was whilst playing rugby for England that Clive developed a very successful career at Xerox and he was passionate about both the game and his business. His experience in managing, leading and motivating teams in the corporate world was not dissimilar to those qualities required of a coach in the sporting world.

On his return from Australia Clive established his own company whilst the world of amateur rugby in England was turning professional. At this point Clive began a serious coaching career in rugby and the recognition of his success at this level, combined with his unique experience outside rugby in both business and education, meant that his CV was beginning to take shape into what would ultimately land him the job as England Rugby Head Coach.

With the dawn of the professional era, there was a requirement to take on a coach with new ideas who could lead the way in developing an England team to be the best in the world. As Clive admits, he was by no means the favourite for the job, but he

Above left: Clive Woodward in his playing days for Leicester in 1984.

Above right: Clive playing for England in 1980.

> "It's not only about skills. It's about attitude and the effect on the team. One wrong player can sap all the energy from the group."

Sir Clive Woodward

knew that with a clean sheet of paper and players turning professional, he could coach, develop and run the team as a business. Managing the revenue streams and the ambition for England to lead the way in this new era were paramount in his mission as the first ever full-time professional coach of the English rugby team. In his first two years as head coach, there were a lot of questions over whether he was the right man for the job. The challenge of transforming the mindsets of amateur rugby players into professionals and introducing new skills and ways of coaching was naturally received suspiciously by a system and players who had known no differently for so long.

Clive knew that, as in business, if he could get through the first 2-3 years in creating a base of success and hold his nerve through the tough times, he was capable of maximising his chance to develop an England side that would compete with the best in the world. With a World Cup falling within the first two years of his leadership, his resolve as a coach was to be tested very early on. A devastating defeat to South Africa in the quarter-finals in Paris was most definitely the low point in his career as England Head Coach.

Clive introduced a lot of changes following this defeat, whilst under huge pressure from the RFU, the media, the players and the public. He had to hold his nerve and believe in his long-term vision and ability as a coach. The tipping point came soon after with a victory against France in Paris and suddenly the momentum was back with Clive; his players began to believe that they really could achieve big things. The pain of the South Africa game was in fact a crucial part of England's journey and ultimately led to four years of unbridled success and the eventual glory of becoming world champions.

As Clive highlights, it takes time to develop a team and individuals. And you earn the respect that you require as a leader from the sheer quality of your actions. Those around you need to believe that you are throwing everything into the job. Investing time in individuals is as important as focusing on the team as a unit. Each individual needs to understand that being part of a great England team is not enough; the aim was to become the best player in the world in his position. Clive knew that if he could create an environment where going onto the pitch he had 10 players who were gold medal winners and could get into any team in the world, they could win the World Cup.

This required huge discipline from each player, to a point where they were so well prepared that, when faced with the ultimate challenge, there were no excuses. Talent alone would not meet this challenge; the ability to take this talent to a higher level is what would make this team and its players special.

Part of Clive's coaching process focuses strongly on the ability of the individual to take on knowledge and learn new things whilst becoming totally absorbed in the process. In terms of the England rugby team, this meant a reorganisation in the way

"Martin Johnson has it. He drives. There's thirty-five seconds to go. This is the one… It's coming back for Jonny Wilkinson…. He drops for World Cup glory… It's up… It's over! He's done it! Jonny Wilkinson is England's hero yet again. And there's no time for Australia to come back. England have just won the World Cup…"

Ian Robertson, BBC Radio Five Live, 22 November 2003

Above left: Clive Woodward holds aloft the William Webb Ellis Trophy as he leaves the field after England's victory over Australia in the Rugby World Cup Final match at Telstra Stadium, 22 November 2003, in Sydney, Australia.

each player took on new information. Some were sponges and eager to learn; others were rocks, stuck in their old ways, and these people, however talented, needed to adapt or be left behind. Clive and his coaching team re-designed their training so that they could measure how much each individual was learning to the point that players were turning up for training at Twickenham eager to know what was to be learned that day.

Thinking correctly under pressure is something Clive believes is totally teachable, with much of his knowledge in this area coming from his experience in the military and in particular from the Royal Marines. As a leader in sport, the military or business, you need to prepare for every possible scenario and to give individuals the best tools possible to cope under pressure. Staging real-life scenarios on the rugby pitch or on the battlefield, as well as in the classroom, prepares and tests each individual to deal with any pressure situation so that they are able to think through their actions when under pressure.

The World Cup Final was a perfect example of this type of pressure. None of the players, coaching staff or Clive Woodward had ever experienced extra time in a rugby

game; it never normally happens. Yet here the England team were in a World Cup Final at 14 points to 14 facing extra time. The fact that this scenario had been prepared and trained for meant that each player knew what had to be done, right down to the drive forwards by the pack followed by the drop goal routine and the huge importance in being the next team to put points on the scoreboard. The drop goal by Jonny Wilkinson, 25 seconds before full time, was one of the greatest moments ever in the history of British sport. The final score was 20 –17. It was this attitude towards preparing and learning in every detail which developed this team into World Cup champions.

Clive is now Director of Elite Performance for the British Olympic Association that supported Team GB in achieving a record haul of medals in the Beijing Olympics. Clive's role is to implement his training techniques to the coaches of the Olympic individuals and teams across all sports. As Clive points out, there was huge success in cycling, sailing and rowing at the Beijing Olympics. In fact, 70% of all the British medals came from these three sports. In the London Olympic Games in 2012, there will be 26 sports represented by Team GB, which means that there are 23 sports in which we are currently underachieving. Clive's role is to fast-track the British teams and individuals to becoming gold medal winners in these sports in 2012. With his passion for developing British talent, there is no better coach to implement this type of challenge; as Clive points out, "you can change the world in four years".

Delivering on the medal table and winning, as in every aspect of Clive's life, are his main drivers in a career that so far has delivered one of the biggest prizes in sport since the 1966 Football World Cup victory, in the form of the Rugby World Cup.

www.olympics.org.uk

Above: England Rugby Union head coach Sir Clive Woodward with England's record trophy haul at Twickenham on 12 March 2004.

Right: Sir Clive Woodward takes his turn at carrying the Olympic Torch through London in April, 2008.

"Champions aren't made in the gyms. Champions are made from something they have deep inside them – a desire, a dream, a vision. They have to have the skill and the will. But the will must be stronger than the skill."

Muhammad Ali

"Leap and the net will appear."

Sahar Hashemi

Sahar Hashemi

Entrepreneur

In 1995 Sahar Hashemi together with her brother Bobby founded Coffee Republic and built it into one of the UK's most recognised high street brands with a turnover of £30 million. Giving up highly paid professional jobs, she as a lawyer in London and he as an investment banker in New York, they staked everything on a dream – and in doing so became two of the main players in the "coffee revolution" that transformed a nation of tea drinkers into one obsessed with "triple decaf lattes".

How they came to build a nationwide coffee chain is a fascinating, courageous and inspirational tale of the ups and downs of following your dream and jumping into the unknown.

The story began when Sahar – disillusioned with her professional life and grieving for her recently deceased father – decided to take a trip to Argentina to learn Spanish. On her way back, she stopped in New York to see her brother. It was in a Thai restaurant in New York that the seed of the idea was first planted. Sahar mentioned to Bobby how much she yearned for New York's skinny cappuccinos and fat-free muffins when back in London. Her brother knew that she was seeking a new challenge after five years as a solicitor in the City. He suggested she look at running her own coffee shops and offered to sponsor her research.

Sahar took up the challenge and spent endless hours in a business library carrying out research and often spent five hours a day getting off at every station on the Circle Line to inspect the existing coffee shops in London.

It took one year to open the first Coffee Republic in London's South Molton Street in 1995. Having been rejected by over 20 major banks, they raised the initial money

Above: Sahar public speaking.

Right: Doodle idea by Sahar for marketing Coffee Republic.

COFEE 200°

← COFFEE BEAN IN FORM OF SIMPLE CARICATURE, SPACESHIP!

STUPID, BUT UNIQUE & EYE-CATCHING & FUNNY!

THEME

THE FUTURE of COFFEE.

NO MORE SHITTY COFFEE.

"Marketing is giving people things they never knew they wanted."

Yves Saint Laurent

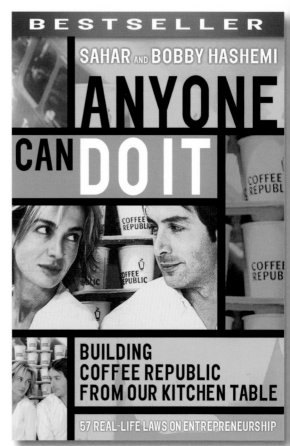

Left: Sahar and her brother Bobby Hashemi, co-founder of Coffee Republic.

Above: Sahar and Bobby's bestselling book *Anyone Can Do It*.

> "Sahar's passion for encouraging innovation energises the room. It is the verbal equivalent of a double expresso from the Coffee Republic chain she co-founded!"

London Innovation Conference 2004

through a small loan-guarantee scheme of £80,000 backed by Nat West. Six months later they raised a further £600,000 from an angel investor and opened a further six stores. In 1997 they took the company public and in four years had succeeded in opening a further 90 coffee bars around the UK. Coffee Republic was named one of the five brands that best represent Britain and in 2002 was named the fastest-growing company in the UK.

Sahar left the day-to-day management of Coffee Republic in 2001 and wrote a bestselling business book entitled *Anyone Can Do It: Building Coffee Republic From Our Kitchen Table*, which tackles some of the fears and answers some of the elusive questions about what it really takes to become an entrepreneur. Sahar believes she is part of a new breed of entrepreneurs who work in corporate or professional environments but who have a burning desire to break away and build the businesses of the future.

Sahar continues to inspire and educate audiences around the world with her story of building a £30-million turnover business and taking on the likes of Starbucks in a revolutionary coffee market. But it does not stop there.

Although Sahar recently declared "There is absolutely no way I will start another business", like any truly driven entrepreneur, she was soon at it again with a new brand of sugar-free candy. The idea behind this venture was very simple: "I have got a sweet tooth but I am always trying to manage my weight". Following extensive research, sourcing of suppliers and sampling, Sahar launched a well-oiled marketing campaign to convince UK consumers that it is okay to eat sweets and cakes – provided that they are from her sugar-free Skinny Candy range. Before long, Sahar and her mother were packing boxes of Skinny Candy at her flat to be distributed to high-end stores such as

How do you define inspiration?

I think inspiration is no one or nowhere specific – it's within you – it almost sneaks up on you when you are on a journey or answering your call- saying "yes" to the call to live the life you want to live – and following your dream – it is an inner power that you activate and awaken by not letting yourself block it – worry, doubt, negative thoughts block inspiration – it is a very powerful force if you learn to unleash it and takes great discipline.

What is your understanding of courage in business?

Courage is not necessarily about risk-taking – it is about staying open, keeping your head down and focused to possibilities and opportunities, so you can act with speed and without conscious reasoning when chance presents itself - that is courage. Courage is about not seeing the future as fixed and not denying our vision and dreams because of insecurity, worry or conscious reasoning - so many people surrender to their worries and just react to outside influences which are totally out of their control. Courageous people realise that worry is just a bad habit of thought – they don't indulge in it – they stick to their inner vision.

What qualities do you admire most in people?

There is an energy that certain people I have met have – it's a childlike quality of being able to wonder – it's extremely and genuinely positive and enthusiastic. It is regardless of age. It is like a momentum and is self-perpetuating. It is a sense of destiny some people have around them – they have an authentic presence. Its exact opposite would be the "victim" attitude. I have heard the words "stay foolish, stay hungry" from Steve Jobs and I suppose these people have this great quality.

What is your biggest achievement in life?

Being able to be myself all day so that my personality, my work and my life are totally aligned – it's a good place to be. I feel I am on a track that has been waiting for me, that is just right for me, living the life I ought to be living. I can be me, my real self, 100% in what I do. So many people don't - they think they need to compromise - I couldn't do it in my first career as a lawyer – now I do it – it's about tapping in to what you love and therefore what you're good at – that I feel is my biggest achievement.

Which areas of your life are you least confident in?

My general rule is if I don't enjoy something or get excited about something I won't be good at it – I feel I am disconnected.

What does the future look like on your landscape, what more can we do, what should we be doing?

So many people make the mistake of seeing a future that is fixed - they have a deep sense of resignation. For me the future is every day – I see it as continually unfolding day by day and not fixed but as a blank canvas to be created every moment by our thoughts and our actions. As a result of those thoughts we go through different mental phases and different desires and aspirations and we need to adapt and adjust our lifestyles to match our mental state – we need to keep flexibility and realise that we are creating the future every moment.

> "Nobody talks of entrepreneurship as survival, but that's exactly what it is and what nurtures creative thinking."

Anita Roddick, Founder of The Body Shop

Harvey Nichols, Selfridges and Waitrose, not to mention branches of Coffee Republic.

This time, Sahar is adamant that she holds on to the entrepreneurial control by keeping the business small and boutique.

"I am deliberately not setting any ground targets. I want osmosis growth where it is steady but there are no limits and everyone can get excited about what might happen in the future"

This new brand is fast developing due to her passion and leadership. Her presence at the recent London Fashion Week ensured that there were Skinny Candy products in the Giorgio Armani goodie bags. Just another of Sahar's many talents!

Above right: Sahar's latest venture, Skinny Candy – a new sugar-free candy range.

www.nspcc.org.uk

"I regard life as being a great adventure full of opportunities and dangers, joys and suffering. I attempt to live it as it comes, one day at a time. I enjoy travelling and in the years of my captivity had an opportunity to take an inner journey which is as difficult and demanding as any exterior journey an individual might take. The years spent totally alone enabled me to gain a better understanding of myself and hopefully a better inner balance. It also enabled me to be less critical of others, especially of those who think and behave differently from myself."

Terry Waite

Terry Waite

Hostage Negotiator

Terry Waite was no stranger to conflict resolution and hostage situations when he was taken captive in Lebanon in 1987 where he remained in captivity for 1,763 days, the first four years of which were spent in solitary confinement.

Having experienced terrible atrocities in Uganda in his early career, he then moved to Rome, where his role was in conflict resolution and the development of public health programmes in war-torn regions around the world. With his career and reputation as an excellent negotiator gathering momentum, he was invited by the Archbishop of Canterbury to join his private staff, based at Lambeth Palace.

It was whilst in this role that Terry Waite really developed his skills as the world's foremost hostage negotiator. He was instrumental in the successful release of seven hostages taken in Iran by the Revolutionary Guard and then in Libya where, through his relationship with Colonel Gaddafi, he secured the release of several British hostages held by a radical group. Terry remembers that at that time all Gaddafi wanted was a better relationship with the West whilst maintaining his image and dignity with the more extreme elements of his country. Alas, this was not to be and many years of terrorist activity were experienced before diplomatic relationships were re-established with Libya.

Terry believes that, in this type of negotiation, you must at the start secure a face-to-face meeting with the captors. If successful, you can then begin to build a relationship of trust to overcome the cultural and religious barriers between the parties. From here a solution can begin to be worked on with the emphasis on all parties leaving the

Above left: Newspaper photographs from January 1987 shortly before Terry Waite was kidnapped.

negotiation with their dignity intact. Terry's strong moral conditions prior to entering into negotiation were that he would not be subjected to blackmail and that no ransom money would be exchanged to secure the release of any captives. Working on purely humanitarian grounds on behalf of the Church, Terry believed that if people were in distress and he could help, then he and the Church should do so.

When the hostage crisis in Beirut first emerged, Terry was not keen to get involved as he was overloaded with similar problems around the world, but was persuaded to do so by the relatives of those kidnapped. Based on his growing credentials, contacts and reputation in the Middle East, Terry was able to get in touch with the kidnappers and meet them personally in Beirut at a time when the city was under siege. One of his main priorities was to establish contact with the right people to ensure this was not a trap to capture him. He was able to do this by asking the kidnappers to tell him the nickname of the girlfriend of one of the hostages. Once they had given him the correct information, Terry went, blindfolded, to a meeting with the kidnappers and discovered their demands, which were essentially for the release of their blood relatives held in a Kuwait prison. He took their appeal and letters as far as the White House, where he met with the US Vice-President of the time, George Bush Senior. Whilst being assured that all would be done to help his humanitarian mission, Terry was unaware of a plot developing behind the scenes. The CIA had backed a private deal with Iran to supply weapons and money to assist in their conflict with Iraq, in return for the release of US hostages held in Lebanon, where Iran were in close financial, military and moral support of Hezbollah.

This, together with the release of a photo to the press of Terry with a high-ranking military US official, Colonel Oliver North, who fronted this operation, ended Terry Waite's credibility in the eyes of the kidnappers. Terry points out that often in a

hostage crisis there is a far bigger political agenda involved in any release of hostages that, as a neutral humanitarian hostage negotiator, you have no knowledge of. Being in direct contact with the kidnappers meant that Terry was under constant surveillance by security services and had to be very careful who he trusted with information, as he was essentially dealing with people's lives.

When the Iran Contra story broke in the press, Terry was faced with a huge decision of whether to walk away or go back to Beirut to meet the kidnappers, knowing full well that the chances of him being killed or captured were extremely high. Out of personal pride and integrity, and to show the captors that he was not shying away and had not broken his word, he decided to go back and renew his faith in the captors and the relationship of trust he had built with them thus far.

The kidnappers saw their opportunity to take Waite hostage and lured him into a trap to see the other hostages. Terry spent the first year under interrogation and was subjected to a mock execution. He was shackled to the wall of an underground cell with no light, allowed out to the toilet once a day blindfolded, and in total solitary confinement for four years.

The first thing Terry Waite did was to refuse food, partly out of anger at his captors but also because he knew that fasting would strengthen his resolve which was key to his survival. Maintaining his identity under this type of extreme pressure was to be the driving force in keeping him sane and alive. He had to learn to live day by day and not look into the future, as well as to accept the past and live with any regrets. With so much time on one's own, the most difficult journey of all was required, an inner journey to get to know oneself better, in order to keep reinforcing one's own identity.

"As a hostage, constantly being kicked around, there is no job, family or friends around to measure your identity against, it has to come from within" – experience has taught him that you have to develop a balanced view of yourself or the risk of becoming

Above left: Meeting the press outside the Commodore Hotel, Beirut, January 1987.

"I have spent four days in the underground prison– at least I think it is four days. The guards will not tell me the time, I can only guess the hour from when they come to take me to the toilet and bring me food. I am allowed one visit a day to the toilet. They have given me a bottle in which to urinate. When they come to my cell, if I need to speak to them they instruct me to whisper. Whenever they knock on my door I must put on my blindfold and keep it on until I am alone and secured behind the locked door."

Terry Waite

depressed and anxious will quickly kill you in captivity. Terry Waite wrote an entire book in his head whilst in captivity and learnt to value solitude, cope with trauma and accept that suffering happens to us all and that suffering need not be negative but can be creative.

Today, Terry Waite still campaigns strongly for Human Rights, particularly for those held at Guantanamo Bay following the Iraq and Afghanistan invasions by the US and their Allies. He believes strongly that we have given a moral victory to the terrorists as their actions have succeeded in leading our great democracies to abuse the basic human rights we have strived to maintain for so long.

"The terrible thing about terrorism is that ultimately it destroys those who practise it. Slowly but surely, as they try to extinguish life in others, the light within them dies."

www.hostageuk.org

What is your understanding of Courage?

There are different forms of courage. There is the courage that faces physical danger with bravery and resolution. There is moral courage that enables the individual to act in a way he/she believes to be correct in the face of ridicule or shame.

What qualities do you admire most in other people?

I suspect that the qualities I most admire in others are the very ones that I lack myself or are certainly in need of considerable improvement. Great compassion – artistic skills – musical ability – love of justice…

How has captivity changed your life?

We live in a world where suffering is a part of life. It cannot be fully understood or explained and is no respecter of persons. The innocent suffer alongside those who might appear to have deserved suffering. I firmly believe that in most cases suffering need not destroy, and that out of suffering creativity can emerge. Although I would not wish to pass through such captivity again, it gave me an opportunity to understand myself better and enabled me to have a clearer focus for my life beyond captivity. I have made a serious attempt to convert the experience into something that can be used positively, rather that thinking of myself as a negative victim. There are some minor physical scars as a result of the experience but they are not significant.

What was the worst time in your life?

Towards the end of my captivity when I was seriously ill with a chest infection and could not lie down. I had to remain seated and chained day and night and frequently lapsed into unconsciousness. There was no medical attention of course.

And your biggest achievement in life?

I never think about that, as when I look around me I see so many people who have made such tremendous contributions to life that anything I might have done pales into insignificance.

What skills are required as a hostage negotiator?

A respect for other people and for ideas and beliefs that are different from one's own. An ability to listen and to understand the position of others. An ability to withstand extreme pressure. An ability to work alone and to take decisions for which one will have to be held responsible. An ability to take calculated risks. Patience and self discipline. Non-sentimental compassion. Sense of humour. There are other qualities but that's enough for a start!

What message do you have for your captors?

I always said to them that I did not agree with kidnapping as a means of achieving a political end but I could understand why they took desperate measures. I would hope that they would work for justice and fair dealing for themselves, their families and their community and reject war and violence as a means of achieving a desired end.

What about the hostage crisis in the world today?

The absolute extremists continue to be few in number although many of the policies adopted by the West have led to an increase in terrorism. I do not underestimate terrorism. It is a grave problem. However, it remains mainly a symptom of much deeper disorders such as social and political injustice; feelings of inferiority and economic imbalance to mention but a few. The actions of the United States of America in breaching fundamental human rights have given extremists an added excuse to recruit impressionable young people into their ranks.

And the future of the Middle East?

Even though I am appalled at the situation in the Middle East I remain an optimist and continue to do what I can to enable men, women and children from all communities to move towards peace and harmony.

Who, where or what inspires you?

I am not the sort of person to wear my faith on my sleeve so to speak but many of my beliefs have developed from my understanding of the social teaching of the Christian Faith. I have a great admiration for the Quakers (Society of Friends), who in a quiet and disciplined way work in the most difficult situations to bring healing and reconciliation to a troubled world.

Right: Terry Waite's first visit to Beirut since his release 14 years earlier.

"Life is not measured by the number of breaths we take, but by the moments that take our breath away."

Miles Hilton-Barber

Miles Hilton-Barber

Blind Adventurer

Miles is a 58-year-old ex-Zimbabwean who dreamed of being a fighter pilot. He joined the Rhodesian Air Force at the age of 18 but had his hopes shattered when he failed his eyesight medical. At the age of 21, he and his brother were shocked to be told they both had a genetic hereditary disease that had jumped several generations and would lead to total blindness. By the age of 30 Miles was totally blind and, as he says, became a "victim of his condition", living a very mediocre life.

It was only at the age of 50, when Miles' brother, now also totally blind, achieved the remarkable feat of sailing a yacht alone with no back-up from Africa to Australia, relying on speech-output technology, that Miles decided to change his attitude and think about what he could do, as opposed to what a blind man cannot do. "The only thing holding me back now," he said, "is 5 inches – the distance between my ears. Attitude is what determines altitude!"

This remarkable man, who has been blind for the past 30 years, has, in the last eight years alone, set numerous records while undertaking extreme endurance events across the Sahara Desert, Antarctica, Siberia, and the Gobi, Qatar and Mojave deserts, with his friend and sighted guide Jon Cook.

Miles has climbed the Himalayas, Kilimanjaro and Mont Blanc, scuba-dived on wrecks beneath the Red Sea, hot-air ballooned over the Nevada Desert, man-hauled a sledge over 400 kilometres across Antarctica, set the world lap record for a blind driver on the Malaysian Grand Prix Circuit and circumnavigated the world using more than 80 different forms of transport. As if this was not enough, Miles recently

"Miles' attempt to be the first blind person to walk to the South Pole is an extreme act of courage, and I have nothing but awesome admiration for his bravery and determination."

Michael Palin

Far left: Miles giving a corporate motivational speech with a picture of his friend and sighted guide, Jon Cook, on the slide behind.

Left : Miles' business card shows him pushing his disabled friend in a wheelchair at the bottom of the Red Sea.

achieved another outstanding world record, undertaking a 55-day, 21,500 km microlight flight more than halfway around the world from London to Sydney, relying on revolutionary speech output technology and accompanied by his sighted co-pilot. He followed this by becoming the first blind pilot in history to fly a sortie of extreme aerobatics in a +600 mph Hawker Hunter jet fighter, accompanied by an ex-Red Arrows pilot, before setting a world speed/altitude record for a blind pilot, reaching Mach 1.4/1,060 mph in a vertical climb to 50,000 feet in around 90 seconds in an English Electric Lightning in Cape Town, South Africa.

All of his projects are now undertaken to raise money for a blind charity, Seeing Is Believing – there are over 30 million blind people in the world who could see if they had the funds. Miles in fact sacrificed being in the *Guinness Book of Records* in order to attend an event in the Middle East which raised the money required for 200 children to see. This shows what kind of man Miles is – as he says, you have to have "vision and compassion" in life.

Miles also talks a great deal about friendship and commitment. There is no better example of these qualities than when, as he was crossing the Antarctic with his friend and guide Jon Cook, he was forced to abandon the journey due to severe frostbite. Giving up was one of the hardest moments of his life, but he charged Jon to continue without him for a further 31 days to plant the blind charity flag at the South Pole. When this amazing story was told at a fund-raising event, such was the level of emotion generated that the very flag raised £53,000 at auction.

Miles believes in confronting one's fears and embracing change – he believes passionately that people should try two or three radical new things a year, so that their comfort zone grows, rather than recycling their negative habits.

www.seeingisbelieving.org.uk

Q&A

Which expedition are you most proud of?
Probably my attempt to be the first blind person to man-haul a sledge to the South Pole from the Antarctic coast – we were stepping into the unknown, not knowing what challenges faced us across crevasses, through white-outs and blizzards.

What would you say to a person with disabilities who dreams of being an explorer?
I would strongly encourage them – their greatest barriers are not within them, or within their dreams, but in people (often their own family and loved ones) placing stereotypical restrictions on them!

How does being blind restrict what you can and cannot attempt on expeditions?
One of my great desires is to push the boundaries of what blind people can do, so I love to experiment, using new technology or, sometimes, just common sense.

What more can we do for blind people around the world?
Blindness is a challenge, not a handicap. If we can, we need to give blind people back their sight – some 30 million people in the world could see, if funding was made available for simple surgery or medical treatment. If they will never see again, we need to give them rehabilitation to restore their independent living skills, then give them inner vision of their great potential. Helen Keller said: "Sight without vision is equal to blindness". How much worse to be blind without vision…

How do you cope with solitude?
I think that all great achievers have the ability to encourage themselves with no outside support. I sometimes have to talk sternly to myself, reminding myself of past achievements. Role models are so important here – other people who have lived inspiring lives, like my blind brother Geoff, sailing alone from Africa to Australia, or Mike McKenzie, my wheelchair-bound, legless, paralysed friend who still lives life to the full and drives a Ferrari! It isn't what happens to you in life that determines your happiness, but what you do with what happens to you in life…

What makes you happiest?
Happiness to me is closely linked to fulfilment, and fulfilment is the product of achievement, not inactivity. One of the happiest times in my life was when I flew the microlite to Australia. My most important relationship is with my God and Creator – He is my Protector and Provider – He is with me on the mountain tops, crossing crevasses in Antarctica, diving on wrecks in the Red Sea, in the baking heat of the world's deserts, when being tossed about in the microlite like a leaf in severe turbulence and thick cloud at 13,000 feet over the Lebanese Mountains, shivering uncontrollably with ice building up on our flying suits and open cockpit, lying on my back in a fighter climbing vertically at Mach 1.4 over Africa, climbing 90 feet up the swaying yard-arms of a sailing ship in the Mediterranean…

How important are friendship and family to you?
Friendship and family are everything of true value in life. I have been married for 32 years to the most wonderful, precious, supportive wife, and we have three great children. My son climbed Kilimanjaro with me and was my sighted guide running across the Gobi Desert in China. He has been with me down the Olympic bobsleigh track in Lillehammer and canoe-racing through the Panama Canal. All three of our children are scuba divers, and it is an absolute joy diving on wrecks in the Red Sea with them! I owe a special debt of gratitude to Jon Cook, my best friend and sighted guide, without whom I would not have been able to live so many of my dreams. "A true friend is someone who sees through you, yet still enjoys the view."

"God would you grant me the serenity to accept
the things in my life I cannot change,
the courage to change those that I can and the
wisdom to know the difference."

Above: Miles climbing in the Alps.

Serenity Prayer, Karl Paul Reinhold Niebuhr

Above: Miles abseiling Table
Mountain in South Africa.

Right: Miles during his 2000–2001
attempt to reach the South Pole.

"Fear is an opportunity for courage, where you unlock your potential by stepping outside what you know."

Miles Hilton-Barber

"Back when I started, there were people saying to me that what I was trying to achieve was not possible and that it would not work – they just thought that I was an eccentric who loves kids, and they became very preoccupied with the way I look and dress. They did not understand the intellectual framework behind Kids Company."

Camila Batmanghelidjh

Camila Batmanghelidjh

Champion of Child Rights

Camila knew from a very early age that she would be working with children throughout her life. Her early childhood in Iran had been in the lap of luxury where she believed every child born was at risk of being kidnapped and needed, at the very least, two bodyguards. She attributed her need for protection to being a child and not to her father's enormous wealth.

Camila also knew very early on that she was quite different from the powerful characters that surrounded her within her family and she quickly developed an interest in psychology and the arts. She suffered several challenging neurological disorders and it soon became obvious that she would not thrive in mainstream education. It was not until she won an international competition in Iran for her paintings that it was recommended she attend a special school in Switzerland to continue her education.

As in her previous schools, Camila soon became popular with pupils and teachers alike due to her huge enthusiasm in wanting to organise the other children for activities and gatherings. However, the perceptual disorders she suffered from hindered her education and it was not until the age of 16, when a teacher discovered that Camila read the clock backwards, that she was sent to a specialist in London and diagnosed with dyslexia and a severe learning disability.

Camila describes her work as a vocation and at the age of 25 she set up her first charity – The Place to Be – providing therapeutic support for children within schools. At the time, this was a revolutionary model of childcare whereby children could refer themselves to support staff without any adult interference. Camila quickly discovered the sheer scale of the abuse and neglect suffered by children, which led to the founding

Above left: Camila at Kids Company.

"For me, adult society's response to the hoodie shows how far we are from finding the long-term answers to put things right. Camila Batmanghelidjh understands. In her new book, *Shattered Lives*, there is an account of a girl whose pastime it was to 'steal smiles', as she put it."

David Cameron, Leader of the Conservative Party

Left and below: Kids painting and playing at Kids Company.

"Camila is truly the Mother Teresa of London. The way she has injected hope into communities around London is an inspiration. On Christmas Day she gave every one of the 800 children a stocking of presents, kindly donated, as well as 5 minutes in a private room with each child whom she seems to know personally. The mutual respect between her and the children is bewildering. I had a wonderfully fulfilling Christmas day at a Kids Company Centre in Camberwell which showed me the value of love."

Volunteer, Christmas Day 2007

of her current charity, Kids Company, 11 years ago in London.

Camila recalls the first day she opened her doors to the youth of Southwark in a disused railway arch in Camberwell. She had to stand back and watch as local teenage boys turned up with bricks and knives and ransacked the centre. She did not react or call the police, she just kept opening her doors. Soon, Peckham's most violent and dangerous teenagers were pouring in, seeking her help. Camila is a realist and acknowledges the danger that she and her staff are under on a daily basis. She has been sent numerous threats and often worries about being snatched into a van or being shot. What keeps her and her devoted staff on the front line is their determination to make the general public aware that this type of violence in children is a public health issue and not a criminal justice issue.

Kids Company supports children with severe behavioural, emotional and social difficulties resulting from significant levels of trauma and neglect. The children often suffer abuse, mental health problems, substance misuse and homelessness. Kids

"Love is all it takes. We aim to return to children their childhood."

Camila Batmanghelidjh

Company aims to restore their trust and provide an environment in which they can begin the healing process, using a carefully designed support system that includes psychotherapy, counselling, education, arts, sports, hot meals and various other practical interventions. On a budget of £4.5 million, Kids Company currently delivers services to 11,925 clients through 33 inner-city schools in London, a drop-in centre at street-level in Camberwell and the Urban Academy, a new educational institute for the over-14s in Southwark.

Camila's mission is to make the public aware that these children are a result of their upbringing and the challenges that they have been faced with. She is the voice of these children, working tirelessly for excellence in the care profession – Camila believes strongly that morality is a by-product of compassion and care.

"If you are a child living with a drug addict, for example, drug dealers could and will burst into the house at any time of night or day. You are always in debt to them. Girls are often violated by the drug dealers at a young age, and pretty quickly the drug dealers want young boys to come and work for them. I've got kids who sleep with knives under their pillows because they do not know what is going to happen in the middle of the night."

Despite the many challenges faced by this inspirationally colourful woman every day, she humbly credits much of her motivation to her staff who she says are 100% emotionally driven and always accountable, above all, to the children. Camila is passionate about excellence and her biggest inspiration is not a person but the design, found on Islamic mosques, which shows one perfect circle repeating itself in exact mathematical divisions into other circles. The pattern symbolises how one great philosophy will evolve repeatedly, and that is Camila's vision for how her own charity should be run.

When asked what is there left to do, Camila, now in her early 40s, guarantees she will not run a camel sanctuary; anything else is possible. In the future, she plans to be reincarnated as a fat goldfish!

www. kidsco.org.uk

Right: Artwork by children from Kids Company.

"On balance I don't know anyone who loves their job every day. Sure, there were bad days for me where it seemed like a meaningless treadmill, but the good days outweighed the bad. Best of all, every four years I got to go to the Olympics with Great Britain on my back, and, what's more, if I did it right, I won. No matter how bad the weather or how hard the training, you could not put a price on that. Competing for your country is an honour and a responsibility; if I could not do it justice, then I would have just pulled the duvet over my head and gone back to sleep. It was at that point I usually got out of bed and went training."

Matthew Pinsent

Sir Matthew Pinsent

Olympian

Matthew went to school at Eton, where from an early age any boy who wants one gets a boat all to himself to row on the Thames. Nobody could say that he wasted this privileged start to his career. By the age of 17 he was already a member of the international junior rowing team and it became clear that, with his growing ambition, he was destined for big things.

After leaving school, Matthew was selected for the senior international rowing team and then, in his first year at Oxford University, he got the opportunity to do a trial in Steve Redgrave's boat. Redgrave, already a two-times Olympic gold medallist, was looking for a new partner to continue his winning formula. The timing was perfect. As Matthew points out, if it had been 10 months earlier or later, he most likely would not have got this chance. Matthew's confidence, ability and strength peaked just when his idol, Steve Redgrave, needed him.

Matthew quickly developed the necessary appetite for training. Training consisted of between four and seven hours a day, seven days a week, no matter what the weather. There is no doubt that you need a special desire to push yourself that hard for so long. Matthew is unsure whether his commitment to training for so long each day came from the discipline he learned at school or whether it was something he was born with, but when he finished his finals at University he knew very clearly, having already won one Olympic Gold, that he was 100% committed to continue to train with Steve Redgrave and to win again at the next Olympic Games. Competing at the Olympic Games is very special, and winning often becomes addictive to athletes. A gold medal

Above left: Winning Gold – Athens 2004.

Right: Bad photo idea with rowing partner Sir Steven Redgrave – "Just slip these on lads. We'll crop out the flip-flops."

"'Who got it? Did you win?' Canadian voices across the water – twenty seconds pass, heart pumping, legs aching, air scorching through the throat. Suddenly the stands off to the left erupt, flags waving. I look up and see they are all Union Jacks. The voices behind me in the boat roar but I can't hear them. It's over, finally over. Tired beyond measure, relieved, proud and overwhelmed I begin to weep into the boat. First quietly, then sobbing, leaning back into Ed's arms."

Extract from Matthew Pinsent's diary on the day of the Olympic rowing final in Athens

Right: Mentally and physically exhausted, Pinsent collapses back into Ed Coode, after just winning Olympic gold against the Canadians in Athens in 2004 in one of history's most memorable rowing races.

is "life-changing", and as Matthew recalls it is enough to motivate you through all those years of training, hardship and preparation. Everyone remembers the Olympic heroes of their youth – Daley Thompson, Jesse Owens, Seb Coe, Mary Peters – largely due to the history and prestige of the Games.

It also takes courage to become a winner: courage to face the fear of possible failure, and courage to accept the sacrifices that have to be made. But Matthew always knew that his potential, matched with Redgrave's experience and strength, meant that they were the best in the field. He found it impossible to imagine how they could row a great race and not win.

Communication was a vital part of the team's success. One of Matthew's heroes is the explorer Ernest Shackleton, a great communicator who was deeply respected by his fellow crew members. There was honest and open debate between the team members and their inspirational coach, Jurgen Grobler. One of Jurgen's approaches, prior to the Athens Olympic Final, was to identify five things that could win them victory, and another five that could cost them victory. Matthew highlights very clearly that if you run out of ideas, especially in an Olympic Final, this can cause panic and you are not going to win a gold medal.

Having won Olympic gold with Sir Steve Redgrave in both the Barcelona and Atlanta Games as a coxless pair, Matthew continued their unbroken run of successes through to the Millennium Olympic Games in Sydney – still with Redgrave but now in a coxless four with James Cracknell and Tim Foster – where he won his third gold medal in a race which secured the crew a very special place in the heart of the British nation.

Then came Athens, where Matthew made Olympic history by becoming one of only

> "Men wanted for Hazardous Journey. Small wages, bitter cold, long months of complete darkness, constant danger, safe return doubtful. Honour and recognition in event of success."

> Advertisement placed in *The Times* by Sir Ernest Shackleton to recruit crew members for one of his expeditions

five athletes to win gold medals at four consecutive Games. He led the Great Britain coxless four to victory over the Canadian World Champions by only eight 100ths of a second. The GB crew of Matthew, James Cracknell, Ed Coode and Steve Williams vied with Canada throughout the 2,000 metre race and with 200 metres to go the Canadians took the lead. Matthew increased the stroke rate and the British boat clawed back to win by inches. At the end neither crew knew who had won until the roar of the British supporters confirmed their victory.

After a year of highs and lows, it was the perfect response to the doubters who had wondered if Britain could win and if Jurgen Grobler had made a mistake by putting Matthew and James Cracknell in the coxless four. Being knighted by the Queen, with his parents present, was a very special and proud moment.

Matthew relates his performance and experience in rowing to everyday life and business, showing the skills required to be a good leader and part of an inspired team. Too often, he says, we see people hiding problems and papering over cracks – that is no way to win. To perform to the best of our ability we need to set ourselves goals, create a plan, motivate each other to get the best out of each team member, think clearly under pressure and above all communicate honestly.

Life now no longer has one single objective to aim for. He has now retired from rowing having fulfilled all of his ambitions and is now turning his hand to journalism and media pursuits. Currently working as a reporter with BBC News 24, he is covering a range of sports from football to horse riding and from rugby to the Beijing and Winter Olympic Games.

www.sparks.org.uk

"Pain is temporary. It may last a minute, or an hour, or a day, or a year, but eventually it will subside and something else will take its place. If I quit, however, it lasts forever."

Lance Armstrong

Jane Tomlinson (tribute)

Charity Fundraiser

Jane was diagnosed with incurable, advanced metastatic breast cancer in August 2000. The disease had spread extensively and the prognosis was for her to survive six months. Over a seven-year period, Jane fought through numerous courses of chemotherapy and various drug regimes despite also developing chronic heart disease.

In the meantime, Jane, a mother of three from Leeds, took on a series of challenges that were apparently impossible for someone suffering from cancer and undergoing chemotherapy, including a full Ironman (4-km swim, 180-km bike ride and full marathon – completed inside 17 hours), two half Ironmans, the London Marathon three times, the New York Marathon, three London Triathlons and three long distance bike rides – John O'Groats to Land's End, Rome to Home and – her final huge challenge – a 6,781.8-km ride across America.

Jane received numerous awards for her efforts including:

- An MBE and subsequently a CBE by the Queen
- The Helen Rollason Award at the BBC Sports Personality of the Year Awards in 2002
- Twice recognised at the Sportswoman of the Year Awards
- A Great Briton Award
- Voted the most Inspirational Woman in Britain in 2003
- A Pride of Briton Award in 2005